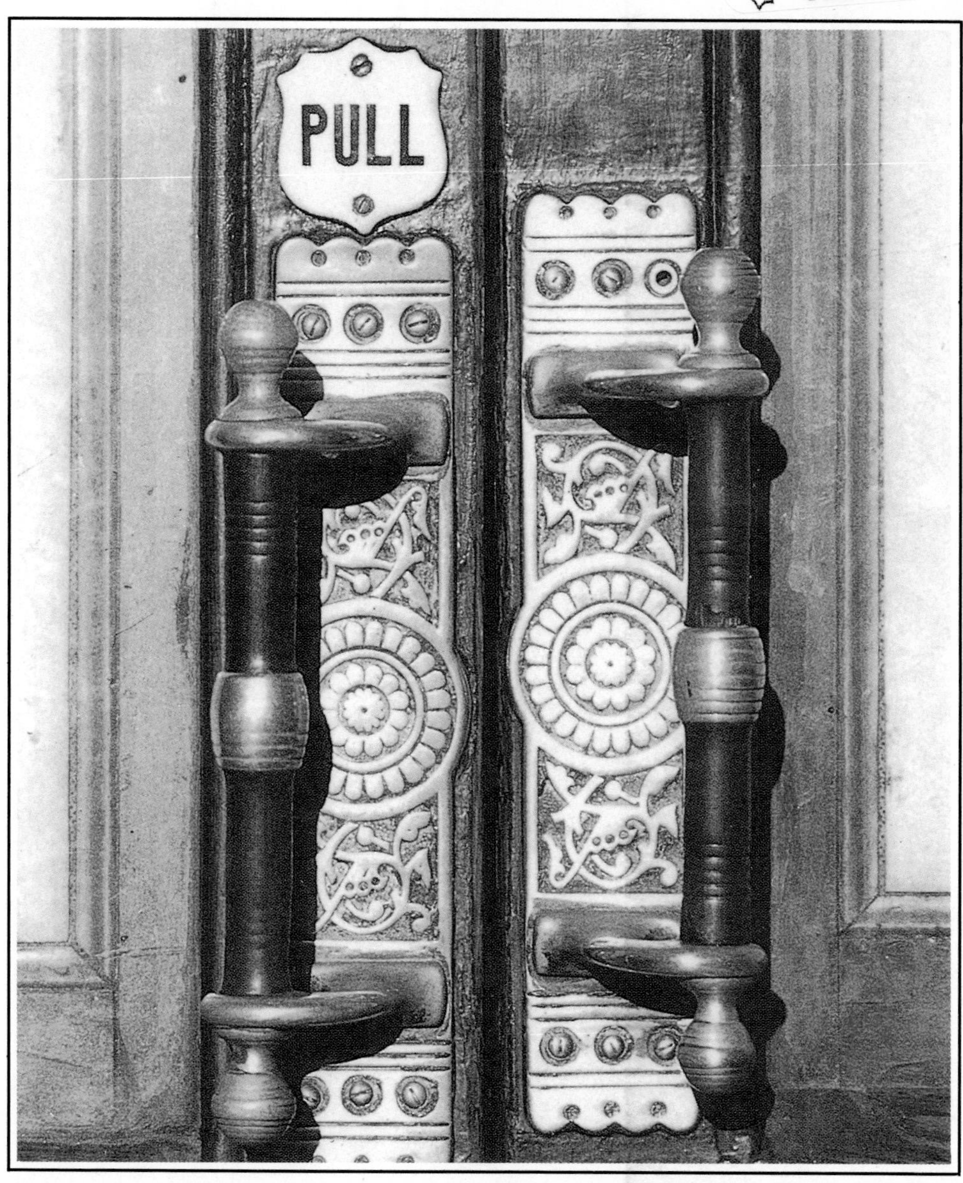
PULL

IRISH PUBS

IRISH PUBS

" When money's tight and is hard to get
And your horse has also ran,
When all you have is a heap of debt
A PINT OF PLAIN IS YOUR ONLY MAN".

At swim two birds.
Flann O' Brien

First published by
© REAL IRELAND DESIGN LIMITED
27 Beechwood Close, Boghall Road, Bray, Co. Wicklow, Ireland.
TEL: (01) 2860799 FAX: (01) 2829962

1985
Reprinted 1988, 1991.
Softback Edition 1993

Photography Liam Blake
Preface and Design Joe Reynolds

Period prints from the 'Lawerence Collection' courtesy The Gallery of Photography, Dublin, also the National Library of Ireland.

Reynolds, Joe
IRISH PUBS
ISBN 0-946887 02 0

Period prints from the 'Lawrence Collection' courtesy The Gallery of Photography, Dublin, also the National Library of Ireland.

PREFACE

The delight in the anticipation of undertaking the production of a book on 'Irish Pubs' has only been superceded by the actual formation of the book.

Gathering the photos together, viewing and selecting the slides, by Liam Blake, and combining the introduction by David Pritchard, and just generally watching the book come together, has given me immense pleasure.

There's something magical about 'Irish Pubs' even when on occasions you find you are the only customer, the atmosphere of relaxation and peace overcomes you, and one almost embraces an element of guilt for taking pleasure in this den of somewhat controversial character.

The walls of so many 'Irish Pubs' have heard stories of great joy and celebration, also those of tragedy and great sadness. They have listened impassively as one might expect, taking neither side of any argument, like the same diplomatic barmen, under those cautious eyes all of human life passes by.

These same men take on a kind of angelic glow as each night progresses, their steady, stalwart, pillorlike strength, earning them titles such as 'Pat', 'Mick' or 'Tom', these are titles not learned easily, for it's in the way in which they are expressed and their timing that matters most.

It is only after one has learnt through perseverance and dedication over a number of visits that this art of capturing attention can be acquired and appreciated.

One can only envy the masters of this art who, sitting at a crowded bar amid shouts for more drink and song, simply say 'the same again Pat', and immediately their request is heard and attended to.

These are just some small observances taken to illustrate, perhaps in a not too articulate way, the kind of soft atmosphere that 'Irish Pubs' accommodate. It would be a pity to lose this part of our tradition and heritage.

One can see with great alarm the threat of this modern age of video games, T.V. and video films, creeping into more and more 'Irish Pubs' as standard equipment.

'Irish Pubs' are in grave danger of losing their essential character should this advancement not be curtailed. Perhaps this book can serve as a salute to their visual colour and charm and also as a reminder of their great preserve.

Joe Reynolds

THE IRISH PUB

There is a story about the monument to Charles Stewart Parnell situated at the top of Dublin's O'Connell Street. The great patriot stands up there on the pedestal, his arm outstretched. Above his head are written the words of his most famous speech, beginning . . . 'No man has the right to fix the boundary to the march of a nation . . .'. It is said that his hand points directly to the door of the nearest public house.

Nobody can deny that the Irish Pub is a unique institution, admired and even imitated wherever emigrants from Ireland have settled. From New York to Sydney 'Irish' bars sell porter and Irish whiskey to people whose ancestry may be many generations removed from Ireland, and yet who seek in such places an affinity with a country they may never have seen. Alcohol drinking is a major factor in the social life of this Island, and the pub plays an integral and very important role in the Irish scene. Which is not of course, meant to imply that all Irish people are drunkards, or even drinkers. The temperance movement has been railing against the evils of the pub for almost a century and a half by now, and hundreds of thousands of Irish people have taken the 'pledge' and refrain from drinking intoxicating liquor of any kind. But even the pioneer must acknowledge that the little Sacred Heart badge in his collar is a response, albeit a negative one, to the central position of alcohol in our society. Whether you love it or loathe it the pub is at the hub of Irish life and to ignore its existence is tantamount to losing sight of the heart of the people.

In Flan O'Brien's famous novel 'At Swim Two Birds' one of the characters recites a poem praising the national beverage . . .

> *" 'But wait till you hear the last verse man, the final polish off' said Shanahan. He frowned and waved his hand . . .*
> *'In time of trouble and lousy strife*
> *You have still got a darlint plan,*
> *You can still turn to a brighter life –*
> *A PINT OF PLAIN IS YOUR ONLY MAN!'*
> (Furriskey, Shanahan's companion, makes a comment)
> *'There's one thing in that poem, permanence if you know what I mean. That poem, I mean to say, is a poem that'll be heard wherever the Irish race is wont to gather . . .' "*
> (from At Swim – Two-Birds by Flann O'Brien [MacGibbons & Kee, 1960])

Despite their reputation abroad, the Irish are by no means the heaviest drinkers in Europe, and the problem of alcoholism, though bad enough is no greater here than it is in numerous other countries. What is unusual, however, is the Irish attitude towards drinking. Traditionally drinking was considered an important masculine attribute, and drunkeness is tolerated to a far greater extent in Ireland than elsewhere. 'In the part of Dublin where I come from' said Brendan Behan, 'it is not considered a disgrace to get drunk. It is regarded as an achievement.' Whatever the reasons for this attitude towards drinking, and they are no doubt complex, the Irish most definitely considered drinking a social occupation for the male only, something to be indulged in outside the home and away from the family. This is why the pub is of such importance in the social life of the country, because, as the gathering place of the male population, it was where the important moral and political issues of the day would be debated and a consensus of opinion arrived at. In this sense the near total exclusion of the female from pub society has had a most harmful effect on the attitude of men towards women in Ireland and it is only with relief that we can see that the pub has lost its status as a male preserve. However, in its influence on public opinion, the pint has been as powerful a catalyst as the pulpit, and the pub is as worthy of serious discussion and consideration as the church.

Before going into details about this neglected part of our national heritage, it is necessary to put forward some sort of working definition as to what constitutes 'a pub'. The Irish Public House, the pub or bar as it is commonly known, is a premises licensed by the government to sell alcoholic beverages to the adult population. Our licensing laws, which control the hours at which pubs are permitted to be open for business, are an adaptation of English laws, changed somewhat over the years to meet Irish conditions. There is still a false notion prevalent outside the country that Irish pubs stay open both day and night, an attitude exemplified by the joke answer to the question 'When do the pubs around here close?', which is 'About September'. In fact the laws concerning closing times are strictly enforced and though 'after hours' drinking still goes on, the overwhelming majority of pubs operate within the legal time limit. In its purest form the traditional pub has grown out of the drinking dens of the people in earlier times and its prime function is to supply intoxicating liquors and a place in which to consume them. In practice, of course, most pubs nowadays sell food and in rural areas they might have a room or two to let for the night, but the essence of the pub is that it is a place where drinking takes precedence over all other activities.

The taverns of Mediaeval Europe, which catered to the needs of pilgrims and other travellers, providing food and accommodation as much as a place to meet and drink, were almost unknown in Ireland, where roads were few and dangerous and travel a hazardous occupation. There are no Irish equivalents, for example, to the ancient foundations along the Pilgrim's Road to Canterbury in England, which so influenced the development of drinking establishments in that country. At a later period Coaching Inns were established in Ireland to serve the coaches which delivered mail and passengers throughout the countryside. The best remaining example of these is the Brazen Head (Plate 1) in Dublin, a fine old building with its own courtyard and reputedly the oldest hostelry in Ireland. But neither the Coaching Inns nor the Hotels which were built during Victorian times to serve the tourist trade to Killarney and other beauty spots, were intended to be used by the bulk of the Catholic population, being erected rather to provide accommodation for mainly English visitors who were already touring the country in considerable numbers.

The pub as we see it today has its peculiarly Irish roots in the nineteenth century, when Dublin was the second city of the British Empire, and brewing and distilling were becoming major Irish industries. The countryside was being opened up by the canals and later the railway and the products of Guinness and other manufacturers were finding markets in areas that hitherto they had been unable to reach. English was replacing Irish as the language of rural Ireland and as part of the policy to make the country adhere to English patterns there was a vigorous campaign against the illegal drinking place, helped along by the Pioneer Movement of Father Theobald Matthews in the 1840's, which resulted in the consumption of spirits being halved within a few short years. As the shebeen and the grog shop declined they were replaced by licensed establishments, where the emphasis was on beer and stout, rather than gin and whiskey, and the new pubs established themselves as the common meeting ground of the people.

Most Irish pubs are privately owned, often over several generations by the same family. In most cases the pub will have either the owner's or founder's name above it and this is far more common than the pub being given a name of its own, though there are exceptions (Plate 2) where a pub will be given a name that refers to some local feature. Oliver St. John Gogarty once made a comment to the effect that whilst the name above the door might change, the pub will remain the same and this is very true in that when a new proprietor takes over a premises he is quite likely to change the name to his own without thinking of making any other alterations or changes in the pub.

In size older Irish pubs tend to be fairly small, ranging from the one room pub so common in remoter areas to the larger and more ornate examples in the city (Plate 3), which have a large bar, plus a snug for the use of women (Plate 4) and possibly one or two private cubicles. Perhaps the most magnificient of Ireland's remaining pubs is the impressive Crown Bar in Belfast (Plate 5), with its magnificent plaster work and carved wooden interior. This pub, which has been restored immaculately by the National Trust of Northern Ireland, is a magnificent example of the skills of the nineteenth century craftsman (Plate 6).In many ways however it is not a typical specimen of the Irish style of pub, belonging rather with the industrial ethos of Belfast in its Victorian heyday, and though Ryans of Parkgate Street might be picked out as a superb Dublin pub of the same era, the Crown Bar has no remaining counterparts elsewhere in Ireland.

The traditional Irish pub varies greatly in its external appearance, depending on its environment and the tastes of its owners etc. but certain decorative motifs give it some uniformity of style. Probably it will have the owner's name written on a board across the top of the window or in very small pubs simply above the door (Plate 7), and the hanging sign (Plate 8) is an uncommon and often modern feature. Particularly fetching are the window displays which are found in the windows of pubs in both city and country, often giving them an almost shoplike appearance (Plate 9). These displays take various forms but standard features are the Whiskey and Guinness bottles placed there to entice the passerby (Plate 10). The very best pub exteriors are works of art in themselves, rich in marble and glass and gold lettering (Plate 11). Utterly different, but equally fascinating in their own way, are the strikingly bright colours which are commonly found on the outsides of country pubs (Plate 12), and occasionally primitive murals on the gable (Plate 20) enhance a whitewashed wall.

The interior decor of the pub ranges from the extreme austerity of the small country pub at one end of the spectrum to the more sumptuous Edwardian interiors of the finest Dublin pubs at the other, but again certain features are common to all. The pub mirror (Plate 14), advertising alcohol or tobacco, is found in most pubs and the example shown in the illustrations to this book is a fine specimen of the type. The counter of the pub is customarily made of mahogany and here are found the 'taps' through which the beer is poured. Draught beer is a fairly recent innovation in Irish pubs and in most of them the beer flows through the little illuminated attachments provided by the suppliers, which advertise the beer that is being sold. But some pubs do possess the old style pumps with wooden handles and these, when they are kept polished and shined, can have a very attractive appearance (Plate 15). The pub clock, usually kept a few minutes fast to encourage customers to leave at closing time, takes various guises, the most typical perhaps being the round faced mahogany version, which in some older pubs is built into the shelves behind the counter. This area, the 'bar' proper, has had the meaning of its name extended to give another term for the pub itself. The 'bar' is the brightest part of the pub and will usually have shelving, with mirrors, bottles and various other bits and pieces (Plate 16). In many older pubs the gas light predated the electric light and a few places still have their original brass lamps, now converted for electric bulbs.

The influence of Guinness, with its distinctive colour, is felt both inside and out. Probably all pubs, old and new have the Guinness sign (Plate 17) on display in one form or another. The various advertising campaigns undertaken by the company over the last fifty years have had a strong effect on the 'look' of the Irish pub. Most commonly seen is the oldest of all the slogans, 'Guinness is good for you' (Plate 18) which dates back to 1929 and has passed into the language as a catchword. The series of animal cartoons by James Gilroy are also found here and there, as in the unusual example (Plate 8) in this book. Sometimes the black and white motif is extended to include the whole exterior of the pub, as in the case of O'Donoghues of Baggot Street (Plate 19), the original haunt of the 'Dubliners' folk group, and this perhaps is ultimately the most logical colour scheme of all for an Irish pub.

The nature of the Irish pub has been very much determined by the development of the Irish alcohol industry and the type of drinks which are consumed in Ireland have had a powerful influence on the habits of the people. 'Whiskey would make a rabbit spit at a dog' says the old proverb and this fiery spirit is perhaps the most uniquely Irish drink of them all. It was first distilled in Ireland well over a thousand years ago by monks who had come in contact with spirit making on missionary journeys through Europe. Unlike their counterparts on the continent, who used wine as a base, the Irish made their distillation from barley and thus invented 'uisgebeath' meaning 'water of life', a tribute to its medicinal qualities. Whiskey became the staple alcoholic beverage of the Irish countryside and remained so right up until the nineteenth century and no doubt its fiery qualities had much to do with the legendary wildness of Irish Fairs, where vast quantities of it would be consumed. Whiskey drinking also contributed to the savagery of the notorious faction fights which were such a notable feature of the period and which were partly responsible for giving the Irish their reputation as violent and pugnacious drinkers.

Pot stilled Irish whiskey is distinguished from its Scottish blended counterpart (spelt without the e) by being distilled three times after fermentation and not twice, as in Scotland. A couple of hundred years ago there were over a thousand legal distilleries operating in Ireland, as well as countless illegal stills producing poitin, an unsanctioned spirit made usually on a potato base (though sometimes barley would be used to produce a cruder form of whiskey). Since then, more rigourous government control, changed drinking habits and the setting up of more economic larger distilleries have reduced this number to the point where one great amalgamated company, the Irish Distillers Group (formed in 1966), controls the distribution of all the whiskeys and other spirits made in Ireland.

It is under their trademark that you will find the great brands of Irish Whiskey which are so much a part of the Irish pub tradition. Whiskey, drunk straight or as a chaser to a pint of Guinness, has always been, by custom, the man's drink in Irish pubs and whilst there are fine Irish made gins and other spirits, they cannot compare in fame to the spirit distilled from barley.

The best known Irish whiskies are probably Powers, Paddy and Jameson. In more sectarian times it was said that you could tell a whiskey drinker's religion by his brand, the Catholics preferring Powers whilst the Protestants went for Jamesons. The oldest of the surviving distilleries is situated up near the Giant's Causeway in County Antrim and has been making whiskey continuously since 1608. Its product, the Old Bushmills brand, is particularly noteworthy and distinctive in flavour. These are changing times, of course and many new and varied drinks are being sampled in Ireland's pubs, but the combination of

JOHN JAMESON & SONS
★ ★ ★
JOHN POWER & SONS
10. YEARS OLD
WHISKEY.
10 & 11.
TEAS
MALT
IS THE
BEST.
BOVRIL
225

Irish whiskey and stout is still a potent and popular one and perhaps the most representative example of the traditional tastes of Ireland's drinkers.

Guinness has become identified with Ireland all over the world. The most important date in the history of Irish brewing is undoubtedly December 1st 1759, on which date Arthur Guinness opened his brewery at St. James's Gate on the banks of the river Liffey. From this first small premises was to grow the great industrial empire that has become so entwined in Irish life and culture and which today sells its beers in over one hundred and fifty countries.

It is a peculiar fact that the porters and stouts for which Guinness's are famous were not originally a native Irish brew. Barley beer is one of the oldest alcoholic beverages known to man, dating back almost to the farming communities of some ten thousand years ago. In Ireland beer was not a particularly popular drink, especially outside of the cities, and the local beers were noted for their sourness and poor quality. The first beers that came from the Guinness brewery were simple ales, but in 1770 a new beer began to be imported from England. It contained roasted barley, which gave it a distinctive dark colour, and since it was particularly popular with the porters at London's Covent Garden, was commonly known as 'Porter'. Guinness, along with several other Dublin brewers decided to try his hand at the new drink; unlike those of his rivals his proved to be a success. By the end of the century, in 1800, Guinness's had switched over entirely to the production of porter and the phenomenal process of growth, which was to make the St. James's Gate brewery the largest on earth by 1900 had already begun.

There are several varieties of Guinness available in ireland, but easily the most popular is Guinness's Extra Stout, sold either on draught or in the familiar yellow labelled bottle. In Dublin, when the first metal containers for draught stout were introduced they were nicknamed iron lungs, which is why you sometimes hear calls for a 'pint of lung' in Dublin's pubs. A huge amount of Guinness is consumed in Irish pubs,

for example in the 1960's over 80% of the beer drunk in Irish pubs was made by the company, and the importance of Guinness in the habits of Ireland's drinking population cannot be overestimated. The pint of stout, drunk either from the old fashioned straight sided pint tumbler (Plate 20), or the more modern handled tankard, is still by far the most common of all drinks seen in Irish pubs despite the trend towards lighter ales and lagers during the last few decades.

There are many reasons for the ongoing popularity of Guinness, most important needless to say being its uniquely rich taste. Guinness lovers span all social classes, from the richest to the poorest. The noted American millionaire and Art collector Chester Beatty, for instance, was in the habit of saying that the only reason he came to live in Ireland was for the Guinness, and even when dining with some of the world's most famous statesmen, he would have a glass of stout in preference to the finest wines. Devotees of Joyce's 'famous ebon ale' seem able to drink it by the gallon. Here for instance is the Welsh poet Dylan Thomas . . . 'Don't you call me morbid George Ring. I remember once I drank forty-nine Guinnesses straight off and I came home on the top of a bus. There's nothing morbid about a man who can do that. Right on top of the bus too, not just the upper deck' . . .

The appearance of a pint of stout is also an appreciable factor in its worldwide appeal. There is something almost ritualistic in the way a good Irish barman will pour a pint of Guinness from the tap, carefully filling it and levelling it until the creamy white collar sits perfectly on the rich black porter, 'the parish priest' as they call it in some parts of the country. Other beers and even stouts are brewed in Ireland, but none can ever compare with the immortal stout made in Dublin by the Guinness family. 'For they garner the succulent berries of the hop and mass and sift and bruise and brew them and they mix therewith sour juices and bring the must to the sacred fire and cease not night and day from their toil, those cunning brothers, lords of the vat.' *(James Joyce, Ulysses [The Bodley Head]).*

In rural Ireland, the pub has evolved along different lines than its counterpart in Dublin and the other cities. By European standards the peasant society of the Irish countryside might have been crude and impoverished, but within its still vigorous fabric were retained the remnants of an ancient Gaelic tradition of music and literature. The secular gathering place of the people was the Shebeen, a primitive and illegal drinking place where poitin and other spirits were consumed in vast quantities. Here would come the wandering performers, whose ancestors had been the bards and rhymers to the great Irish Lords before the wars of Elizabeth I had destroyed the native aristocracy. In the shebeen there would be story telling and recitations by Gaelic poets and wild dancing to the fiddle and pipes, played in a style whose origins went back to the remotest times. The Itinerant musician had an important secondary role as the gatherer and dispenser of news and as he moved through the countryside he would keep the seperate communities in touch with each other and with developments at home and abroad. Rural society, in religion Catholic and in language still mainly Irish speaking, was a closed book to the English who ruled the country. Between the peasantry and the Protestant landlord class, there was an innate hostility and an impenetrable wall of mistrust hid the inner life of the rural masses from their colonial oppressors. The Irish peasant, isolated and excluded from power, responded to foreign domination with the blank stare and the secret society.

Some residue of this deep rooted secretiveness still permeates the atmosphere of the country pub. Hospitality to the stranger was one of the concepts at the root of ancient Irish society and the visitor will find nobody more generous or kinder than the people he might chance to meet in a country pub. Yet at the same time he may become aware of a curious shynes in those he meets when it comes to discussing local affairs, so unlike the Dublin pub where your fellow drinker will reveal the most private affairs of his closest friend to you without batting an eyelid. This reticence creates a boundary which the outsider cannot and should not penetrate and whilst the visitor may catch a glimpse of the inner life of a rural community in its pub, only after a long residence in the area will he be fully admitted into its society.

In modern times, of course, Irish society has been revitalised and the countryside is more alive than it has been for many generations. But the destruction caused to rural Ireland by the Great Famine of the 1840's was beyond measure and it is arguable that its effects are still visible today. The immediate deaths by hunger were terrifying enough in themselves, but even more damaging were the effects of emigration and depopulation which emptied the countryside and sapped the will of the people. The late marriage became customary and often in the farming family these younger sons who did not emigrate would remain batchelors so that land holdings would pass on to the next generation undivided. The beautiful Irish countryside, once so alive and full of children, became a land of lonely middle aged men and deserted farmsteads.

The masculine predominance in rural life has left a strong mark upon the country pub. In pre-famine times records indicate that women mingled freely with men in Irish drinking places. The intoxicated woman was a common enough sight and there is an old folk saying 'a drunken woman knows no shame' condemning such behaviour. However in the late nineteenth century a strongly moralistic tendency in the Catholic Church imposed new standards of strict behaviour on the Irish people and the idea of women and men drinking together came to be considered improper and even indecent. The pub became a male preserve where women were not allowed to enter. This is reflected in the snug, a partitioned off area usually near the door, where women would be tolerated, provided they did not enter the main body of the pub. In Dublin where the influence of the church was never quite as strong as elsewhere, this unspoken rule was not always strictly adhered to. In the male orientated batchelor society of the West, however, where women were more vulnerable to social condemnation, the male

Chas Cook
ART PHOTOGRAPHER
ENTRANCE TO
STUDIO THROUGH THE BAZAAR
Photo Materials
RE-BUILDING Must Clear
THE BAZAAR
W. WATERS
WILLIAM WATERS
WATCHMAKER
JEWELLER & OPTICIAN
PHILIP. P. HYNES & Co. TEA WINE & SPIRIT MERCHANTS
No 1. TEA
P. P. HYNES & Co.
TEA, WINE &
SPIRIT MERCHANTS
PURE MALT WHISKY
DEWAR'S
PERTH
WHISKY

dominance of the pub became absolute and the older pub had no place for women in it. Even today it is possible to walk into a pub on some Atlantic peninsula and find you are sharing the bar with a couple of dozen men, mostly middle aged and all wearing their overcoats, and not a woman in sight.

In one sense, the numerous laws controlling drinking, brewing and distilling introduced by the English government may be seen as part of an attempt to subdue and anglicize the Irish people and to break up their culture and replace it with English standards of behaviour. To a point they were largely successful in this policy, as the disappearance of the Irish language indicates. Against this the notable part that the country pub has played in keeping Irish music alive through the long years of neglect must be noted. That so much of this great tradition is still with us is a tribute, both to the resilience of Irish rural life and to the efficiency of the country pub as a retainer and transmitter of the values and heritage of the countryside. In this context we need only mention the towns Milltown Malbay and villages of West Clare, and the pubs of Milltown Malbay or Doolin, which nurtured the great musicians of that region. In recent years, the revival of interest in Irish music has brought many young people to the West of Ireland to seek out the authentic sources of the music, and a dying tradition that seemed on the verge of extinction has been given a bright new lease of life. One of the most heartening sights at the numerous Music Festivals that have sprung up in Ireland of late, is to enter a small pub and see some old traditional musician passing on his skills to a young, and quite often foreign, afficianado. We must thankfully acknowledge the important role of the country pub in rescuing traditional music from the anthropologist and the Folklore Archive and giving it back to the people.

The true country pub, as befits its descent from the shebeen, tends to be on average smaller and more spartan in its fittings than its cousin in Dublin and the larger towns. Ellens Pub (Plate 21), a little thatched pub in a remote part of County Sligo, gives a particularly good idea of what the shebeen might have looked like, and with its fine local musicians has much of the un-inhibited atmosphere of earlier times. The older unrenovated pub will as often as not consist of no more than a small room, with a mahogany counter and a few wooden tables and chairs. Decorations will be minimal, quite possibly consisting of no more than a few inconsequential pieces of bric-a-brac and an old calendar or print on the wall. The austerity of these old pubs has led to suggestions that they indicate some inbred feelings of guilt on the part of the Irishman about his drinking habits, that drinking was less of a sin if carried out in uncongenial circumstances so to speak. However, this seems over fanciful and the probable truth is simply that economic conditions were such that publicans could not afford to spend money on decorating their premises and making them more comfortable.

Pubs are sprinkled around the countryside in profuse numbers but more remarkable is the number of pubs found in the small market towns, where it is not uncommon to find three or four licensed premises together in a row (Plate 22). Often the pub will have a dual function, being also a hardware shop (Plate 23), a Post Office, or even an undertakers (Plate 24). These drinking places exist to serve the farmers of the surrounding areas, as well as the people of the town. The pubs are especially busy on market days, when local farmers come in to buy supplies and to trade cattle and other livestock. In addition to filling their traditional role as a place for a quiet drink when the day's work is done, at these times country pubs become an unofficial office for the trader and the farmer, where they can bargain and complete their deals with a handshake and a thirst quenching pint of stout. Gossip and information are exchanged with the cattle dealers and other merchants who come in from outside the region for the fair, so that even in this age of television and the daily newspaper, the pub still retains some of its quality as a window on the outside world.

Many of Dublins famous old pubs date from Victorian times, when

Dublin was becoming a fair sized city, a little seedy perhaps in comparison to the days of its Georgian glory, but with a large popularion (including an English garrison) who needed places to mingle and to drink. The very best of these pubs are still reminiscent of this period, Mulligans of Poolbeg Street for instance (Plate 25), with its Joycean memories and unspoilt decor. Despite her ghastly slums and notorious red-light district, for the most part Dublin was a relaxed and friendly city and the various sections of the population mixed freely within the doors of her pubs and hotel bars. In this cosmopolitan city, with its witty and eloquent proletariat, the pub developed into a neutral ground where class distinctions could be dropped and good conversation indulged in as an end in itself. Tom Corkery writes about this tradition as he saw it continued on into the 1950's. 'Yet the poet could and did share the same pub with the peasant and no man had need of looking up, down, or askance at his fellow man.' Patrick Kavanagh could be heard discoursing in McDaids of Harry Street on such esoteric subjects as professional boxing, the beauty of Ginger Rogers, or the dire state of Gaelic Football in Ulster. Flan O'Brien could be heard in Nearys or in the Scotch House on any subject known to man. Brendan Behan could be seen and heard everywhere.' (from 'Tom Corkery's Dublin' [Anvil Books]).

In Dublin's egalitarian pubs it is not only poets who congregate but also the docker and the civil servant and the factory worker and the doctor. The term 'Literary Pub' sometimes seen in tour guides to the city is fallacious, since in any good pub members of every trade will be found, and even in the pubs associated with them, the writers will only be one clique present amongst many. Having said this there is a unique and lasting relationship between the city's poets, novelists and dramatists and her pubs. To illustrate this, here are quotes from poems about the city by three Irish writers.

> 'A public house to half a hundred men
> And the teacher, the solicitor and the bank clerk

81. JAMES McDONNELL. 81
IRONMONGE
T&MA

In the hotel bar drinking for ten'

(from 'Dublin Made Me' by Donagh MacDonagh [in 'The Hungary Grass', Faber & Faber, 1947])

'And porter running from the taps
With a head of yellow cream'

(from 'Dublin' by Louis MacNeice [Collected Poems, Faber, 2/e Rev. 1979])

'Go into a pub and listen well
If my voice still echoes there'

(from 'If Ever you Go to Dublin Town' by Patrick Kavanagh
[Collected Poems, MacGibbons Kee, 2/e Rev. 1972])

The pubs of Dublin have a quality about them that owes much to their clientele. The Dubliner has a character and a way of talking uniquely his own. The city's distinctive dialect has a turn of phrase peculiar to itself and its store of emotive slang words give the conversations overheard in Dublin pubs a remarkable fluidity and richness. Brendan Behan must be noted as the writer who, above all others, was able to catch the Dublin speech and use it for literary purposes. A great pubman himself, he was known all over the city, but the pub most associated with him is MacDaids in Harry Street (Plate 11).

This little piece from 'The Big House', in which two old women in a pub are discussing their dead soldier husbands, displays his mastery of the Dublin dialect.

(Granny Growl) And me first husband was et be the Ashantees. All they found of him was a button and a bone.

(Granny Grunt) Gods curse to the hungry bastards.

(Granny Growl) But still an' all ma'm what business had he going near them. Me second husband had more sense. He stopped in the militia and never went further than the Curragh for a fortnight.

(Granny Grunt) Maria Concepta, do you remember when we used to wait for them coming off the train at Kingsbridge and they after getting their bounty money and waiting in on the station to be dismissed.

(Granny Growl) Deed and I do Teresa Avila and me provoked sergeant, he was an Englishman, would let a roar that'd go through you . . .

(Granny Grunt) That's the very way he used to shout. It used to thrill me through me boozem.

(Granny Growl) Poor ould Paddins, me tired husband.

(Brendan Behan, 'The Complete Plays' [Methuen 1960])

James Joyce wrote about many of Dublin's pubs in his works. The Scotch House, now alas knocked down, is the setting for the short story Counterparts, in 'Dubliners'. In 'Ulysses' there are references to various pubs around the city centre. Most are changed utterly since 1904, or, like Barney Kiernan's in Little Britain Street, now demolished. Of the pubs of Ulysses only Mulligan's of Poolbeg Street, Burke's in 1904, can be said to have remained comparatively unchanged since Joyce's time and it remains now, as then, a simple working man's pub.

Looking at the pubs of Ulysses reminds us how rapidly Dublin's pubs are changing. In the capital, the face of the pub has been evolving for many decades. The expansion of the suburbs over the last forty years has led to the founding of many new pubs and the restoration of many older establishments. Whilst these larger pubs, which have usually added a mixed Lounge to the traditional 'Men-only' Bar and the snug, are more comfortable in their surroundings and sometimes attain to its interesting facades of their own, they lack the character of the earlier premises which are sadly becoming rarer as the years go by. Only when we fully realise that the traditional pub has an intrinsic historical and artistic value of its own, can we hope to see the destruction cease and by then one fears it might be too late.

POWER'S
ESTD
P
1791
WHISKEY

Door Handles, Doheny and Nesbitt, Baggot St., Dublin.

The Brazen Head. Famous 18th. Century Inn in the heart of Dublin City, reputed to be the oldest pub in Ireland. PLATE NO. 1

Marble City Bar. Superb pub front of the Marble City Bar in High Street, Kilkenny. PLATE NO. 2

Doheny and Nesbitt. Fine pub front in Baggot Street, Dublin. PLATE NO. 3

Mulligan's of Stoneybatter. An interior shot showing 'snug' in background. PLATE NO. 4

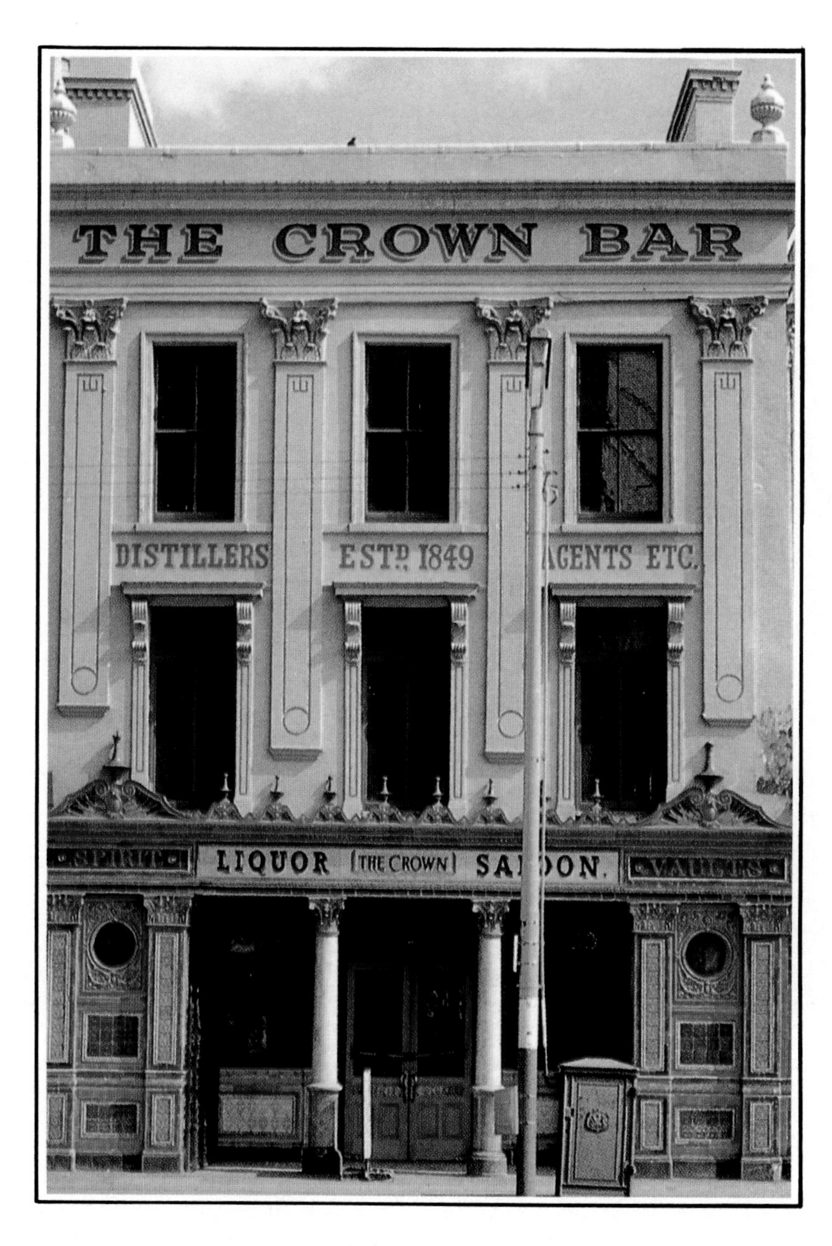

The exterior of the Crown Bar, Belfast. PLATE NO. 5

Detail of tilework, the Crown Bar, Belfast. PLATE NO. 6

Blackbirds, Clonakilty, Co.Cork. PLATE NO.7

" Old fashioned Guiness sign". PLATE NO. 8

Kennys Country pub, Lahinch, Co. Clare. PLATE NO. 9

Martin B. Slattery. Ornate exterior of a pub in the Dublin suburb of Rathmines. PLATE NO. 10

McDaids of Harry Street, a Dublin pub famous for its literary associations. PLATE NO. 11

Dan Foleys. The brightly coloured front of Dan Foley's, in Annascaul, Co. Kerry. PLATE NO. 12

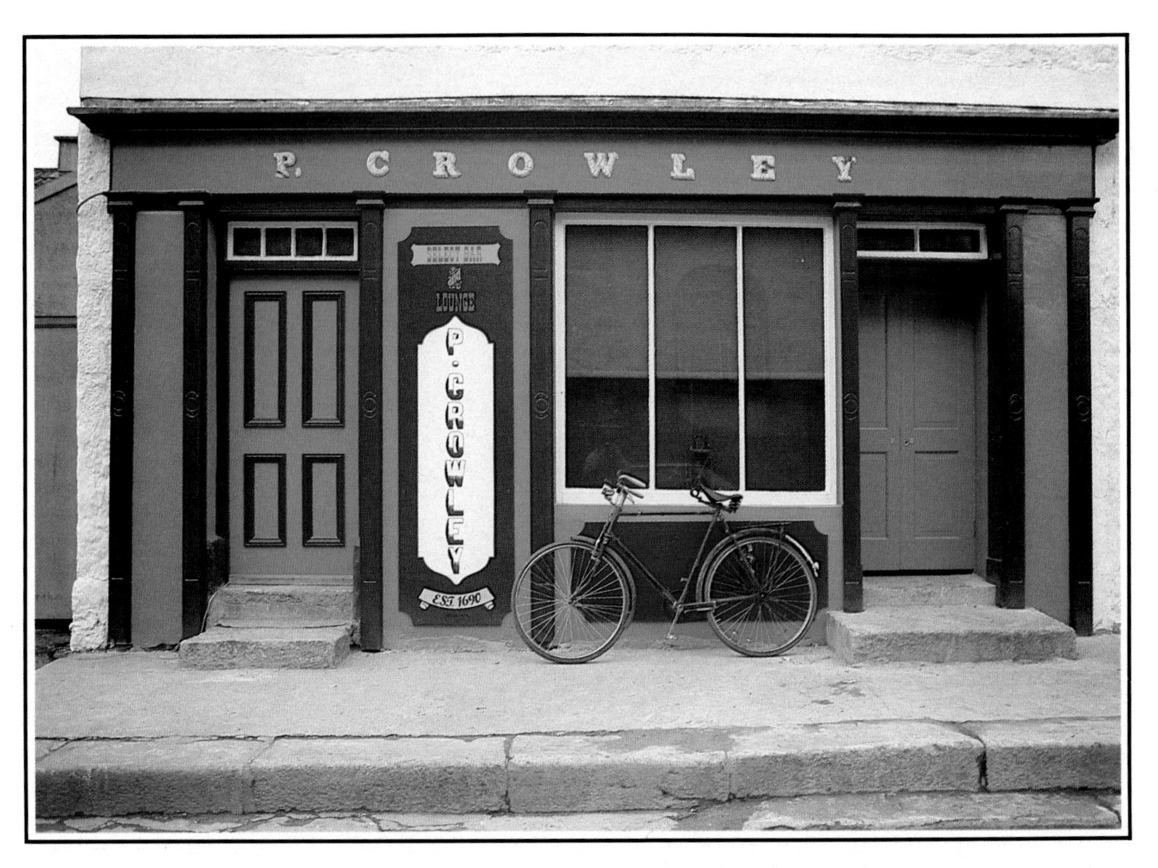

Crowleys. A small pub in Corofin, Co. Clare. **PLATE NO. 13**

Exceptionally ornate mirror in a pub in Dingle, Co. Kerry. PLATE NO. 14

Beer pumps in Ryans of Parkgate street, Dublin. PLATE NO. 15

The bar of Slattery's, Rathmines, Dublin. PLATE NO. 16

THE GREY HOUND
The Grey Hound
STOUT
STOUT

A Guiness sign on the wall of a pub in Donegal. PLATE NO. 18

O'Donoghues. This pub in Dublin's Baggot Street is well known for its associations with Irish folk music. PLATE NO. 19

PLATE NO. 20 Painted advertisement on the gable of a pub in Glengarriff, Co. Cork, showing the old style straight sided pint glass.

Ellens Pub. This thatched pub in Maugherow, Co. Sligo, is particularly reminiscent of the country pub of much earlier times. PLATE NO. 21

Ennistymon, Co. Clare. A row of pubs in a town that is famous for the number of licensed premises it contains. PLATE NO. 22

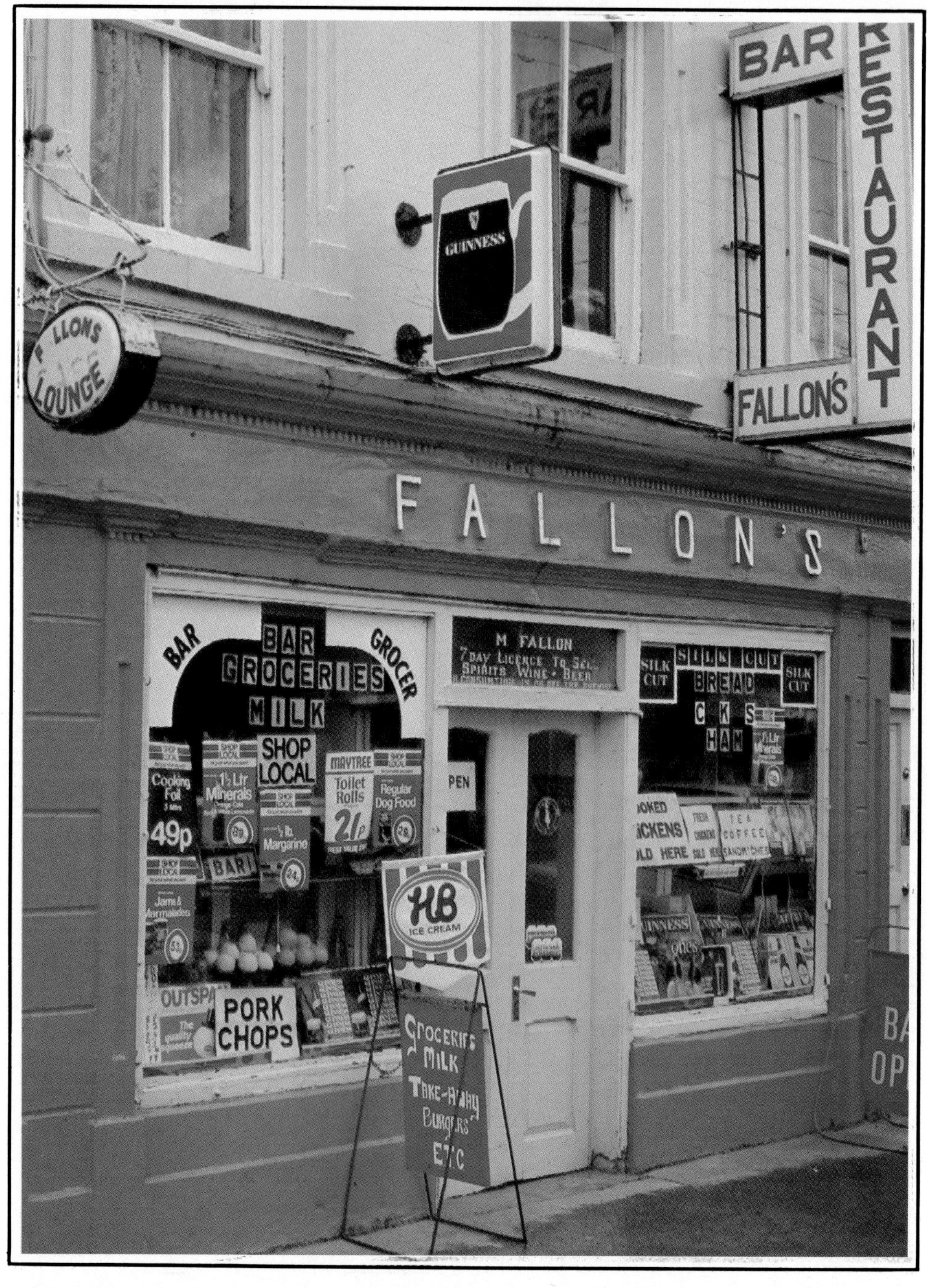

Fallons a strikingly bright facade of a Pub/Grocery in Claremorris, Co. Mayo. PLATE NO. 23

Fox. An extraordinary window display in a pub/undertakers in Navan, Co. Meath. PLATE NO. 24

Mulligans of Poolbeg Street. Shutters up outside of one of Dublin's best preserved old pubs. PLATE NO. 25

John Delaney. A country pub, near Faugheen, Co. Kilkenny. PLATE NO. 26

PLATE NO. 27 Cartlands. Pub/Hardware shop in Kingscourt, Co. Cavan.

Morrissey. A pub in Abbeyleix, Co. Laoise. PLATE NO. 28

P. Cullen. A Pub/Undertakers in Rathdrum, Co. Wicklow. PLATE NO. 29

John Kavanagh. A pub in Glasnevin, Dublin, with an especially attractive front   PLATE NO. 30

T. O'Loughlin. A pub in Dun Laoghaire, Co. Dublin. PLATE NO. 31

M. J. Byrne. A small pub in Grenane, Co. Wicklow. PLATE NO. 32

The Ould Plaid Shawl. A modern sign on an old pub in Kinvara, Co. Galway. PLATE NO. 33

Con Macken. Undertakers Pub in Wexford Town. PLATE NO. 34

Frawleys. Pub in Lahinch, Co. Clare. PLATE NO. 35

James Griffin. Pub front in Trim, Co. Meath. PLATE NO. 36

John Gibney. Pub in the village of Skerries, Co. Dublin. PLATE NO. 37

C. Hayes. Another of the small pubs of Ennistymon, Co. Clare. PLATE NO. 38

John McCabe. Pub in Nobber, Co. Meath. PLATE NO. 39

James Griffin, Ennistymon, Co. Clare. PLATE NO. 40

Tynans Bridge House. A distinctive pub in the town of Kilkenny. PLATE NO. 41

M. O'Shea. Unusual thatched pub in Faugheen, Co. Kilkenny. PLATE NO. 42

Noel P. Smyth. A pub in Haddington Road, Dublin. PLATE NO. 43

John Shaw. Pub in Summerhill, Co. Meath. PLATE NO. 44

Cooneys. An unusual modern facade on a pub in the Dublin suburb of Dun Laoghaire. PLATE NO. 45

Lawlor's Railway House. Small pub in Rathdrum, Co. Wicklow. PLATE NO. 46

Nolans. A tiny country pub in the village of Union Hall, Co. Cork. PLATE NO. 47

M. O'Brien. 'Iron lungs', the metal barrels used to transport Guinness, lined up outside of a Dublin pub. PLATE NO. 48

Donegans. 'Best Ales in Prime Order', an attractive pub front in Collon, Co. Louth. PLATE NO. 49

Wm. Moloney. A country pub in Co. Kilkenny. PLATE NO. 50

Anderson. Pub in Ardee, Co. Louth. PLATE NO. 51

Clearys Bar. A neon sign illuminates the traditional facade of this pub in Amiens Street, Dublin. PLATE NO. 52

Hanrattys Bar. Pub in Carrickmacross, Co. Monaghan. PLATE NO. 53

O'Connell. Pub in Richmond Street, Dublin. PLATE NO. 54

Gibbons. Old pub in Neale, near Cong, Co. Mayo. PLATE NO. 55

Old stained glass windows are an interesting feature of the modern interior of Kitty O' Shea's, Dublin. PLATE NO. 56

Hennessy. Pub in Ferbane, Co. Offaly. PLATE NO. 57

O'Shea's. Pub front in Sneem, a small village on the Ring of Kerry. PLATE NO. 58

Courtney. The distinctive green facade of this well known pub in Killarney, Co. Kerry. PLATE NO. 59

The House of McDonnell. Pub in Ballycastle, Co Antrim. PLATE NO. 60

Nolans. Pub in Birr, Co. Offaly. PLATE NO. 61

Stacks. Pub in Ennistymon, Co. Clare. PLATE NO. 62

Powers Whiskey Mirror, O'Connell's Pub, Richmond St., Dublin. PLATE NO. 63